The Call of the Birds

For Nic and Bruce, who made it possible for me to write this book surrounded by the birds of New Zealand.

Séraphine Menu

For the kingfisher, the robin and for all those that go 'cheep-cheep'.

Fleur Oury

Published in the USA in 2025 by Post Wave Children's Books,
an imprint of Post Wave Publishing UK Ltd,
Runway East, 24–28 Bloomsbury Way, London, WC1A 2SN
www.postwavepublishing.us

First edition 2021
Published with permission of Albin Michel Jeunesse
Original title: *Oú Sont Passés Les Oiseaux?*
Written by Séraphine Menu and illustrated by Fleur Oury

www.albin-michel.fr

10 9 8 7 6 5 4 3 2 1

ISBN 979-8-89509-022-0

Printed and manufactured in China by Leo Paper Products,
Heshan, Guangdong. June 2025.

MIX
Paper | Supporting responsible forestry
FSC® C020056

The Call of the Birds

How We Can Help Birds Everywhere

Séraphine Menu & Fleur Oury

Translated by Michele Hutchison

post wave

FASCINATING BIRDS

Birds have always captivated men and women alike. Their **plumage**, their song, and their flight patterns have intrigued scientists as well as artists, farmers, and romantics. Mysterious and free, birds were also the inspiration for humankind's craziest project: learning to fly ourselves.

Ever fascinating, birds feature in fairy tales, legends, and folklore. Humans even invented a mythological bird—the phoenix—which is the color of fire, can burst into flames and then rise again from its own ashes. We also tell children that storks deliver babies!

To this day, bird references form a part of our everyday lives. The owl is a symbol of wisdom, a swallow can signify the arrival of summer, and a raven is a bearer of bad news. Someone who is cheerful is said to be "as happy as a lark," while a person who can't stop talking is sometimes said to be "as talkative as a magpie."

But birds are more than just the symbolic traits attributed to them. Magpies, for example, are not only "talkative," they are also incredibly sensitive. When one of them dies, they hold a kind of funeral ceremony.

Albatrosses are also sentimental: they remain faithful to the same partner all their lives. Carried by their immense wings, these seabirds fly tens of thousands of miles across the oceans, but always return to spend the mating season with their partner.

And what about starlings, who "dance" in the sky? Every evening, as they search for a place to roost, thousands of individuals come together to perform a synchronized dance, possibly to deter any **predators** in the area. These huge swarms of starlings—known as "murmurations"—offer a breath-taking spectacle to those lucky enough to come across them.

Albatrosses and starlings are not the only birds who regularly leave one part of the world for another. Half of the world's feathered population do this. Birds often fly to warmer climates for the winter and return to their original habitats in the spring to breed. This is called migration.

There are many different types of migration: a nightingale travels in stages, with many breaks, while a swallow can travel 600 miles without stopping.

Young wild geese rely on their parents to show them the way, while a cuckoo makes its way alone once it has left the nest.

For **migratory birds**, life in the sky is made up of cycles, of departures and returns, and journeys that end and then begin again. But in recent years, fewer and fewer birds have been returning to the Northern Hemisphere in the spring. The countryside is growing quiet, the forests are deserted, and the cities seem populated by just a few different species. So, where have all the birds gone?

HUMAN MEETS BIRD

EARLY EXTINCTIONS

The relationship between humans and birds has not always been peaceful and poetic. Over the centuries, numerous human activities have threatened the sky's population. Hunting and **poaching** in particular have led to entire species being wiped out.

The New Zealand moa is one such example. These enormous birds grew up to 12 feet tall and weighed about 550 pounds, but they couldn't fly, so by the 15th century they had been hunted to the point of extinction.

The dodo is the first bird to become extinct in recent history. Up until the 17th century, these large birds lived on the island of Mauritius, where there were no predators. But since they too couldn't fly, they were easy **prey** for European explorers

landing on the island. Every last one of them was hunted down and eaten, or their nests were destroyed by pests that were introduced by the settlers.

Today, other island birds, such as the New Caledonian kagu and the New Zealand kiwi, are still endangered because they live on the ground. Their predators are no longer people, but our pets—cats especially.

BIRD BULLETIN:

In Lewis Carroll's famous novel, young Alice meets a dodo in Wonderland.

EXTINCT SPECIES

Great auk

Hoopoe starling

Mascarene parrot

Spectacled cormorant

Huia
Hawai'i 'ō'ō
Carolina parakeet
Alaotra grebe

WHEN BIRDS BLOTTED OUT THE SUN

In 1914 the last American migratory pigeon died at Cincinnati Zoo. This species, also known as the "passenger pigeon," had pointed wings, a slender body, and plumage much more colorful than the urban pigeons we know today. It was once so common in North America that millions of these pigeons would gather to migrate.

In the 1810s there were almost three billion passenger pigeons in the United States and Canada. Witnesses from that time described how the sun would be blotted out of the sky when a flock of these pigeons flew by, just like during a solar eclipse! And yet, a century later, these once numerous birds had all but disappeared.

It was mistakenly believed that the passenger pigeon could not be eradicated due to its enormous numbers. Hunting parties were organized, and only hunters who shot more than 30,000 birds were paid. Farmers, who believed the birds were a threat to their crops, caught them in nets or set their habitats on fire. In less than a decade, the passenger pigeon population had disappeared from the wild.

BIRD BULLETIN:

The American migratory pigeon is often confused with the carrier pigeon, which still exists. However, it is not the same species: the carrier pigeon is a common pigeon (also known as a rock dove), trained to carry messages on its legs.

AN ISLAND PLUCKED BARE

Laysan, a small island in the Hawaiian archipelago, was once home to a large number of rare and beautiful birds, including black-footed albatrosses, great frigatebirds, red-tailed tropicbirds, and masked boobies. More than 10 million birds inhabited this area of just 1 ½ square miles.

But in the early 20th century, the birds of Laysan suffered a terrible fate. Hunters from the United States, France, Britain, and Japan arrived in large numbers to kill them. In the space of two years, 300,000 birds were slaughtered. Unlike in New Zealand and Mauritius, these hunters didn't want to eat the birds.

What they wanted was the birds' droppings (known as "guano"), which they could trade as a **fertilizer**. The hunters also harvested feathers as these had become a fashion accessory in major Western cities in the 20th century.

BIRD BULLETIN:

The island of Laysan was home to so many birds that the Hawaiians called it "Kau," meaning "egg." Today, the island still lives up to its name. Thanks to conservation measures, its large bird population has been restored.

BIRDS THAT FELL PREY TO FASHION

By the late 19th century, hats were in fashion. Tall and extravagant, they were often covered in ribbons . . . but also in real feathers. In order to satisfy their customers, **milliners** from Paris, London, and New York competed to be the most creative. Hats were prized for their originality—in some cases, whole stuffed birds were mounted on top of them!

To make sure they could supply milliners with feathers of the best possible quality, hunters shot the tropical birds during the breeding season, when their plumage is at its most beautiful. The birds were killed without having had time to reproduce, and their numbers dwindled year by year.

Birds with brightly colored feathers were sought after, including Chinese egrets, birds of paradise, and pink flamingos. During that period, hundreds of thousands of them were killed each year to decorate the heads of women, but also men, who wore feathers in their military caps.

BIRD BULLETIN:

In the early 20th century, birds of paradise feathers were in such high demand they became more valuable than gold!

BIRD WATCHING

Until the late 19th century, killing and stuffing birds (known as **taxidermy**) was practically the only way for humans to observe them up close and gather scientific information. Some hunters were actually nature-lovers, fascinated by **biology**.

It was the invention of photography in the mid to late 1800s that changed the fate of our feathered friends. For the first time it was possible to record information about a bird without harming it. Instead of being stuffed and displayed in a **cabinet of curiosities** or a museum, the bird could now be studied in its natural habitat.

Many hunters put down their guns and grabbed a camera instead. The first photographs showed birds eating, nesting, or bathing. Photographing birds gave people a new interest in them.

BIRD BULLETIN:

Photography proved that the grey-bellied cuckoo (like many other cuckoos) was a ***parasitic*** *bird. Instead of raising the chick itself, the cuckoo lays its eggs in the nests of other species so that its young can be fed by foster parents. Often, the newly hatched cuckoo chicks dispose of the other eggs or chicks in the nest!*

ORNITHOLOGY TAKES OFF

Over time, the desire to protect birds increasingly outweighed the desire to hunt them, as people became more interested in living birds than dead ones. **Ornithology**, the science of studying them, took off.

Scientists began to observe birds, either for research or to satisfy their curiosity. They studied their feeding habits, their mating behavior, and the rhythms of their migration. Ornithologists had to be patient and discreet, sometimes having to wait a long time to observe birds in their natural habitats, so as not to run the risk of disturbing them.

From the early 20th century, every Christmas Eve many farmers in Scandanavian countries such as Sweden, Norway, and Denmark, would leave a sheaf of wheat in their gardens as a gift for the birds. This tradition was encouraged among children and marked the start of changing attitudes toward birds. Around that same time, the first **nature reserves** were established in the United States to protect wildlife.

BIRD BULLETIN:

The bald eagle was once in decline, but thanks to the nature reserves created in the United States, its population has been able to find places to thrive. Without this intervention, Americans would probably have lost their national bird!

WHERE HAVE THE OTHER BIRDS GONE?

The extinction of the dodo, the American migratory pigeon, and several indigenous species from Laysan took place quite a long time ago. The fashion for feathered hats is over, and hunting—though not gone—has less impact on the winged population than it used to. People are more sensitive to the plight of animals and have learned to protect them.

But even though attitudes have changed, birds are still disappearing—and in increasing numbers. Today, it is not only the rare, tropical, and already endangered species that are declining in number, but also more common birds such as robins, sparrows, and swallows.

During the last 50 years, 3 billion birds have disappeared from North America and 500 million from Europe. Asia, South America, Africa, and Oceania also show worrying losses. Why are birds continuing to disappear like this?

FROM THE AIR TO THE GROUND

A WHOLE WORLD UNDER OUR FEET

Everything in nature is well designed. Every animal, plant, and organism has its place in the web of life. From the biggest blue whale to the smallest **bacteria**, every living thing is important.

The natural world is made up of **ecosystems**: ordered environments in which living things evolve. Savannahs and oceans, to name but a few, are ecosystems. Within each of these, there are both prey and predators. These animals form part of a **food chain**: a logical sequence in which each animal feeds and, in turn, serves as food.

For example, blue tits need caterpillars, caterpillars need plants, and plants need soil to survive. Under the ground, there are millions of microscopic bacteria and fungi that make life possible. The other links further up the food chain, such as birds, depend on them. The population of the sky wouldn't exist without everything that lives in the ground!

BIRD BULLETIN:

Birds have a huge variety of feeding habits. There are carnivores (meat-eaters) such as the falcon; omnivores (everything-eaters) such as the crow; piscivores (fish-eaters) such as the kingfisher; insectivores (insect-eaters) such as the blue tit, and granivores (grain-eaters) such as the sparrow. Life on Earth forms the basis for all of these different diets!

THE FOOD CHAIN

In the food chain, animals eat plants or other animals to get energy. At the bottom of the chain are producers—organisms, such as plants, that can make their own food. At the top are predators. The arrows on this diagram show who eats what.

Buzzard
Blue tit
Plant
Caterpillar

WHEN HUMANS GO TOO FAST

Earth's ecosystems have evolved very slowly, over hundreds of millions of years. This slowness is part of life's natural cycle, because living things can only evolve and adapt to their environment little by little.

But humans have accelerated the evolutionary process. Our progress is now too fast for nature to adapt at the same rate. In the 19th century, the effects of human intervention on our planet had greater consequences than ever before. The population grew, and with so many more people on the planet, cities expanded, and more blocks of apartments, factories, and industrial parks were built. These changes disrupted entire ecosystems.

To feed this ever-growing human population, small farms gave way to large industrial enterprises. Great expanses of land were devoted to a single crop, a practice known as "**monoculture**." This new form of agriculture led to the destruction of many hedgerows and the disappearance of meadows and scrubland—all places that birds call home.

THE WAR ON INSECTS

The practice of monoculture meant that entire acres became dominated by one type of crop. As a result, certain species of insect started to multiply, causing problems for farmers. An insect that feeds on wheat will rapidly increase in number in an area where only that cereal crop is grown.

During the Second World War, humans greatly expanded their understanding of chemical weapons. Once the conflict was over, this knowledge was used to destroy insects. **Insecticide** entered our homes and our fields.

In the 1960s, the American biologist Rachel Carson became concerned about the effects of these chemicals. In her book *Silent Spring*, published in 1962, she explained that DDT, a powerful insecticide used widely by farmers, had led to the disappearance of many insects, and, at the same time, birds. It emerged that, alongside other side effects, DDT affected birds' reproductive systems, made their eggshells too fragile so that chicks could not survive, and poisoned many species, among other side effects. The book caused an uproar and DDT was banned in the United States in 1972 (with a few exceptions).

BIRD BULLETIN:

Due to the high levels of DDT present in the prey it ate, the peregrine falcon became almost extinct in many countries by the 1970s.

BIRDS OF THE CITIES, BIRDS OF THE FIELDS

Even after DDT was banned, robins, tits, partridges, and swallows continued to disappear. Across the European countryside, insecticides called "neonicotinoids" are still causing a lot of damage. They trigger the death of insect pollinators (such as bees and butterflies), and other insects, depriving certain birds of their food.

When ingested by migratory birds, the chemicals affect their thyroid glands—the hormone glands that allow them to gain weight before the winter. In order to migrate, birds need to gain weight. If they are too weak, they cannot fly to faraway places or return from them.

In urban areas, other problems arise. Major cities with high-rise, modern buildings do not provide the small holes and spaces where **urbanites** such as sparrows like to nest and shelter. Air pollution from car fumes also has a negative impact on bird health, in addition to other detrimental factors.

In capital cities such as Paris, Berlin, and Rome, pigeons have multiplied more than they should have. They have adapted to an urban lifestyle and feed on anything and everything, including the contents of trash cans or scraps left on outdoor café tables.

BIRD BULLETIN:

In recent years, it appears that storks have shortened their migration route. Instead of heading to Africa from northern Europe, they settle in southern Europe near garbage dumps, where they feed on trash.

TOURISTS AND BIRDS

When humans aren't directly affecting nature by changing its landscapes, we sometimes affect it indirectly, by moving around ourselves. Tourism, a relatively recent activity in human history, has transferred millions of people to parts of the world that were previously unvisited.

Iceland, one of the most popular destinations of the 2010s, has suffered greatly from tourism. Only about 330,000 people live in this remote landscape, but in 2017, it welcomed more than two million tourists—six times more than its population!

The Atlantic puffin, also known as the "sea parrot" or "clown of the seas" because of its colorful beak, is a seabird found only in the cold waters of the North Atlantic.

In Iceland, it likes to nest on the ground and hide in tall grass. But since the arrival of tourists, puffin colonies have been destroyed because their environment has been changed and damaged by increased footfall in its habitat. The species is also threatened by pollution and **climate change**, which **mass tourism** contributes to.

A SUFFERING CLIMATE

For more than a century, the world has been warming up. Everywhere on Earth, rising temperatures are causing areas to dry out, resulting in the loss of watering places for birds, among other things.

Saharan oases—green spots in the middle of the desert that serve as stopping places for birds on their migration routes—are gradually drying up. This means that migrating birds have to travel longer distances without being able to stop and rest.

But it isn't just watering holes that are affected. Global warming is wreaking havoc with nature more widely. The life cycles of many plants and insects are linked to temperature. Changes in the weather can cause them to emerge before migratory birds have returned from their long winter journeys, or outside of the breeding season, which can impact how and when the birds feed and nest.

BIRD BULLETIN:

According to organizations who monitor and protect the yellow-eyed penguin (a fish-eating bird that lives only in the south and southeast of New Zealand), the species has fewer and fewer fish to feed on. The penguin's ocean has become so warm, many fish species have stopped swimming there.

THE BUTTERFLY EFFECT

There were no rabbits in Australia before Europeans introduced them in the 18th century. Since these small mammals had no predators, they multiplied so rapidly they wiped out natural vegetation and destroyed much of the continent's crops in a short space of time. To solve the problem, the Australians tried all kinds of things, including introducing viruses to eradicate them. But the birds of prey who ate the rabbits were, in turn, poisoned.

This story shows that any change in the balance of an ecosystem can have a series of unfortunate consequences. When humans interfere with one of the links in a food chain, the whole chain can be thrown out of balance. This scientific

phenomenon, in which a small disturbance can cause major changes, is known as the "**butterfly effect**." For a long time, humans saw nature as something they could influence without consequence. In reality, humans are part of the living world: we *are* nature! So, by opting for a new relationship with the natural world, might it be possible to save the birds?

REPOPULATING THE SKIES

THE BIRD THAT NEVER REALLY DISAPPEARED

How do we know for sure that a species no longer exists? In New Zealand, the takahē, a bird with blue and green plumage and a large red bill, was considered extinct for 50 years before specimens were suddenly spotted again! In the late 19th century, British settlers who had colonized the islands reported seeing a few of the birds, but as scientists found no trace of them, they presumed the species was extinct.

A New Zealand doctor and bird-lover called Geoffrey Orbell doubted this. He thought that a few individuals may still be living in a region known as Fiordland, a wild and inaccessible area where narrow stretches of water are surrounded by mountains. In 1948 he decided to go on an expedition in search of the takahē.

Just as he had imagined, Orbell found two takahēs on one of the mountain peaks. But the scientists refused to believe him, and so he had to return with a new team in order to be taken seriously. It was later believed that the takahēs had found refuge in Fiordland after humans arrived on the island, and had been able to survive because they were so isolated. Unfortunately, the species is still considered endangered today and is on the International Union for Conservation of Nature's Red List. There are fewer than 500 left.

A RESCUE FROM PESTICIDES

Native to Japan, the crested ibis is a large white bird with a red head, which feeds on small fish and shrimp that are found at the edge of **rice paddies**. **Pesticides** used in rice **cultivation** from the 1960s onward gradually led to its disappearance. In the 1970s, the crested ibis was considered an extinct species.

In 1981, however, seven crested ibises were found in a remote province in China. The birds had been able to survive there because no pesticides were used in the area. The Chinese government organized their rescue and created a reserve to allow the birds to live and reproduce in a favorable environment. Despite this positive outcome, the species is still threatened with extinction.

The sarus crane, the world's tallest flying bird, has undergone a similar rescue in Vietnam in recent years. When its population plummeted after being poisoned with pesticides, an area was set aside for the birds in the Mekong Delta—a vast labyrinth of swamps, islands, and rivers. The environment is conducive to protecting many bird species.

ORGANIC FARMING

Like the takahē, the crested ibis, and the sarus crane, many birds can only live in isolated places or areas that are free of chemicals, where non-aggressive farming practices are used.

Some farmers are aware of this and are turning to more sustainable ways of producing food that are also more harmonious with nature. **Permaculture**, for example, is an **organic** method that takes inspiration from natural processes and respects living things. It has even made it possible to restore **biodiversity** in areas that were totally barren!

Farmers who choose to farm their land organically aim to take care of the soil, forests, water, and all other living things present in the environment. For them, there are no "weeds" or "harmful" insects. Everything that exists can coexist, as long as the natural balance is respected.

MAKING CHOICES

It may seem strange, but our **consumption** habits—that is, what we decide to buy day after day—affects the fate of birds. Even the most trivial everyday questions such as, "What shall we have for dinner tonight?" have repercussions for the bird population and the entire planet.

The Amazon rainforest, which covers over 2 million square miles of South America, is home to some 40,000 plant species, 3,000 fish species and over 1,000 bird species. In fact, around a tenth of the world's birds lives here. But as a result of human activity, thousands of acres are being destroyed every year in order to grow soybean and palm oil. Macaw, toucan, and hummingbird populations are declining as their territories are shrinking.

Buying food containing palm oil or meat from animals fed on soy, means unwittingly encouraging the cultivation of products that destroy the Amazon rainforest and cause the disappearance of these birds. So, our daily choices matter: by buying different food, we can reverse the trend!

LITTLE THINGS COUNT

You can save birds by changing your eating habits, but also by making a few simple gestures. For example, if you live in the countryside, you can increase the amount of water available to wildlife in your garden. Scientists estimate that since 1900 the Earth has lost around 65 percent of its wetlands. Yet these wetlands are essential for living things, including birds.

We now know that to protect birds we must first protect insects, and also the microscopic creatures, plants, and fungi that live in the soil. We can learn how to care for living things at each stage of the food chain by respecting nature and understanding that every living thing has a place.

If you live in the city, there are other things you can do, such as getting together with your neighbors to create green spaces for birds in the courtyard of your building (if you have one). Balconies and windowsills can also be used as valuable shelters: all you need to do is build or buy some **birdhouses**.

OBSERVE WITHOUT DISTURBING

Some people install bird feeders to provide food for birds in winter. This is a well-intentioned initiative, but it can sometimes lead to more competition between birds, with some species thriving to the detriment of others.

Instead, indirect actions, such as conserving soil quality or thinking about the consequences of what we eat, can be more beneficial to birds. Each decision we as humans make should try to consider the needs of animals, not just our own motivations. This way, we can restore our relationship with nature.

Intervening directly with nature in general can be tempting, but the best way to care for living creatures is by not getting in their way. The natural world keeps itself in balance, with species regulating themselves and adapting to their surroundings. It is up to us humans to find our place alongside them.

By feeding birds or by trying to tame them, we deprive them of their independence and therefore their freedom. A bird is a wild animal, just as a tiger or crocodile is. There's no more reason to care for or domesticate birds over other species. To protect nature, we need to be as discreet as ornithologists and observe without disturbing!

LET'S ALL BE ORNITHOLOGISTS!

To prevent the extinction of birds, we can all do our bit independently, but we can also come together! It is by coming together—for example through joining bird conservation organizations or participating in group efforts—that we can gradually prevent the loss of birds and make a greater impact.

One example is to join a bird watch association. In most countries, there are regional groups that organize bird counts and monitor wildlife, and they always need new members! To participate, all you have to do is count the birds in your area and report your observations. This is known as "**participative science**": a method in which many volunteers from the public contribute to a scientific cause.

But before engaging with birds, we should get to know them. Learn to observe, to recognize, and to be amazed by them. There is no secret technique: just grab a pair of binoculars, go outdoors and be patient. Take notes or photos, share and tell others. By doing so, the future of the sky can become more populated than ever. It doesn't matter if you are an expert or a beginner, big or small: we can all be ornithologists!

GLOSSARY

BACTERIA: Microorganisms consisting of a single cell. Bacteria are found almost everywhere on Earth, including in our bodies. There are millions of different species.

BIODIVERSITY: All the living things on Earth, including fungi, plants, and animals. Biodiversity evolves over time, as certain species appear and disappear, and environments change.

BIOLOGY: The scientific study of living things, including an organisim's behavior, means of reproduction, diet, and natural environment.

BIRDHOUSE: A specially designed house where birds can come to breed, nest, and rest.

BUTTERFLY EFFECT: An expression that describes how a small disturbance can lead to much larger disturbances elsewhere.

CABINET OF CURIOSITIES: A place where rare objects, natural elements, scientific or artistic creations are displayed, forming a small collection of the "wonders of the world." Cabinets of curiosity were very popular in the 17th and 18th centuries but were gradually replaced by museums.

CONSUMPTION: The process of using, buying, or eating something.

CLIMATE CHANGE: A change in the typical weather conditions of a region over a period of time. This can include global warming, increases and decreases in temperature, droughts and excessive rainfall.

CULTIVATION: In agriculture, cultivation is the act of preparing the land for the growing and raising of crops.

ECOSYSTEM: A set of living and non-living organisms and the environment in which they live. Ecosystems describe how these organisms interact.

FERTILIZER: A natural or artificial substance that helps plants to grow.

FOOD CHAIN: A series of organisms which depend on each other for food.

INSECTICIDE: A natural or chemical product used to kill insects.

MASS TOURISM: A travel-related phenomenon in which a very large number of people visit the same place at the same time.

MIGRATORY BIRDS: Birds that fly long distances between their breeding and wintering grounds.

MILLINER: A person who designs or makes hats.

MONOCULTURE: The practice of growing just one plant species at a time on a farm.

NATURE RESERVE: A protected area subject to regulation, where plant and animal species are protected.

ORGANIC: Natural or related to nature. Food that is grown organically does not use artificial pesticides or fertilizers.

ORNITHOLOGY: The scientific study of birds including their habits, behavior, and way of life.

PARASITE: A living organism that depends on another to survive. It may live inside or outside the host body on which it is parasitic.

PARTICIPATIVE SCIENCE: When non-scientists, such as volunteers from the general public, participate and contribute to a scientific cause.

PERMACULTURE: The agricultural practice of using land and resources in a way that does not damage or alter the environment.

PESTICIDE: A chemical substance that is sprayed on plants to kill weeds, pests, and diseases.

PLUMAGE: The layers of feathers covering a bird's body.

POACHING: The act of illegally fishing or hunting wildlife.

PREDATOR: An animal that feeds on another animal.

PREY: An animal that is eaten by a predator.

RICE PADDY: A water-covered field in which rice is planted and grown.

TAXIDERMY: The practice of stuffing and preserving dead animals, mainly for scientific study or display (for example as part of a museum collection). Taxidermy was very fashionable in the 19th century.

URBANITE: A living creature who lives in a city or a town.